The Best Friends Game Book

Sterling Publishing Co., Inc.
New York

Library of Congress Cataloging-in-Publication Data available

10 9 8 7 6 5 4 3 2 1

Published by Sterling Publishing Co., Inc.
387 Park Avenue South, New York, NY 10016
© 2004 by Sterling Publishing Co., Inc.
Debra Spina Dixon, Illustrator
Excerpted from *Oodles of Doodles* © 2003 by Mike Artell; *Get Out* © 2001 by
Orange Avenue, Inc.; *Super-Colossal Book of Puzzles, Tricks & Games* © 1978 by
Sterling Publishing Co., Inc.; *Zany Rainy Days* © 2000 by Hallie Warshaw; *Sleepover
Cookbook* © 2000 by Hallie Warshaw; *Quick-to-Solve Brainteasers* © 1996 and 1967 in
Argentina and Spain by Juegos & Co., S.R.L, and Zugarto Ediciones under the
titles *Para Resolver en el Autobus* and *Para Resolver en el Ascensor*; *Totally Beads*
© 2001 by Sonal Bhatt; *The Little Giant Book of Science Experiments* © 1998 by
Sterling Publishing Co., Inc., published by Ravensburger Buchverlag Otto Maier
GmbH under the titles *Spiel—das Wissenschafft* © 1964, 1995; *Der Natur auf der Spur*
© 1972, 1995; *Geheimnisse des Altags* © 1977, 1995; *World's Best Card Games for One*
© 1992 by Sheila Anne Barry.
Distributed in Canada by Sterling Publishing
^{c}/o Canadian Manda Group, One Atlantic Avenue, Suite 105
Toronto, Ontario, Canada M6K 3E7
Distributed in Great Britain and Europe by Chris Lloyd at Orca Book
Services, Stanley House, Fleets Lane, Poole BH15 3AJ, England
Distributed in Australia by Capricorn Link (Australia) Pty. Ltd.
P.O. Box 704, Windsor, NSW 2756, Australia

Sterling ISBN 1-4027-1105-0

Contents

How Do You Doodle?

How do you doodle? It's easy, and you probably do it a lot. A doodle is a simple cartoon that people draw when they're talking on the phone or listening to a boring speaker. Doodles keep your hands busy without making your brains work too hard.

The great thing about doodles is that they can really improve your drawing skills and your ability to think creatively. You don't have to be a great artist to be a dynamic doodler. All you need is a pencil and something to write on.

Ready to go? Good! Call someone on the phone, start talking, and get yourself doodling!

Anchors

Draw this shape.

Add a "J" and a backward "J."

Draw some points on the ends of the "Js."

Underwater scenes look more realistic when you add an anchor.

Braces

Draw a smiley face. Show lots of teeth. Add little squares on each tooth. Connect each of the squares with a line.

Wouldn't it be funny if animals got braces on their teeth? Animals like beavers and sharks would sure look weird with braces.

Cheese

Draw a triangle.

Add sides and a bottom.

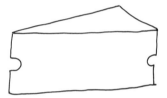

Now all we need are a few holes.

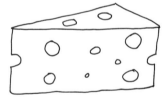

Looks like it's time for a snack.

Crying

Draw tears coming from the eyes. Turn the mouth down at the ends. Add a little wavy line under the mouth.

Whoa! This girl is REALLY crying.

Diapers

Diapers look a little like triangles with two bumps on the top two points. Most of the time, you'll draw diapers on little kids . . .

but sometimes it looks funny to draw diapers on little animals.

Eyes

Here are a few kinds of eyes: pretty, simple, worried, scary, impatient, and wacky.

Try drawing a face four times and change the eyes each time.

Fish

Draw an oval. Add a mouth and eyes.

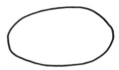 

Add a tail fin. Finish by adding fins on the top and bottom of the fish. Bubbles make the fish look as if it's underwater.

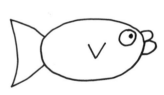 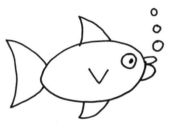

Just for fun, try drawing unusual-shaped bodies for your fish.

Frogs

Frogs start out as a smiley face with legs.

Add a body and two big back legs.

"Kiss me and I'll become a prince."

Guitars

Draw this shape.

Add a neck for your guitar.

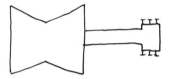

Now draw strings and pegs.

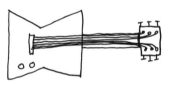

Acoustic guitars are more rounded. Here's how to draw an acoustic guitar.

Hair

Every now and then, draw really weird hair on your cartoon characters. It's funny!

Sometimes hair is so long that it covers the cartoon character's eyes. HA!

Noses

Noses can be round, pointy, short, broad, or tiny. Try drawing some of these noses.

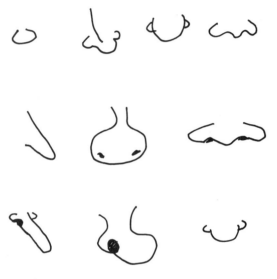

Usually it's best to draw tiny noses on children. Larger noses work best on adults.

Rabbits

Start with a round head, a Y-shaped nose and some eyes.

Step 1.

Step 2.

Step 3.

Draw the same rabbit smaller several times and you'll have a mama rabbit with her bunnies.

Teeth

You can draw teeth that look like windows . . .

or teeth that are round
on top and bottom.

Or weird teeth.

Sometimes goofy
characters have
just a couple of
teeth showing.

Great Games

What kind of games do you like to play? Whatever kind it is, you'll find it here—from blowing bubbles to bashing balloons, from writing your own lyrics to performing the songs you've written, to putting on your own musical revue, with costumes and props.

Here are grown-up twists on children's games: creative games that really stretch your imagination, and acting-it-out games that give you a chance to show off your talent and your sense of humor. Plus, there's a hilarious version of Musical Chairs without chairs. You'll want to play these great games at parties, at sleepovers, and anywhere else when you want to have fun. Take a look!

Blowing Bubbles

OF PLAYERS: **1** OR **more**

You want good clean fun? Nothing is cleaner—or much more fun—than a homemade soap-bubble factory. Here's how to build the biggest bubbles ever in your own giant bubble maker.

YOU NEED:
>   dishwashing soap
>   water
>   bucket
>   twine or string and scissors
>   drinking straws
>   glycerin, sugar, corn syrup, or gelatin (optional)

1. Make a batch of bad-tasting bubble juice in a bucket by mixing 1 measure of soap to 10 to 20 measures of water. Sudsier soap and drier days both require more water.

2. To make bubbles so sturdy that they bounce, add glycerin (available at drug stores), sugar, corn syrup, or gelatin to the mix. Start with about a tablespoon of any of these for every cup of bubble juice.

3. Build your bubble maker. Cut a piece of heavy twine or cotton kite string about 3 feet long. Thread it through 2 drinking straws and tie a knot to form a loop. If you are using the bendy kind of straws, cut off the ends that bend.

4. Dip the loop in the bucket of bubble juice. Using the straws as handles, open the loop and blow gently on the soap film. Squeeze the loop shut to help form a complete bubble. If you swirl the bubble maker in the air, you'll get funny-shaped bubbles.

TIP:
You can even blow bubbles with your bare hands. While your friends are trying the giant bubble maker, make a circle with your fingers (like the finger sign for "okay"), and dip it in the bubble juice. You should be able to blow bubbles from the soapy film inside the circle. For giant-sized handmade bubbles, dip both hands and make a big circle with your thumbs and pointer fingers.

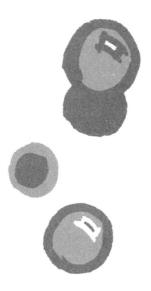

Balloon Shoot-Out

OF PLAYERS: **2** OR **more**

YOU NEED:
> balloons of various sizes
> string for tying

Blow up and tie off 6 balloons—3 for each player. The two players stand back to back and then walk 3 paces. On the count of 3, they turn around and start firing. The object is for each shooter to hit the other with a balloon before being hit.

It's okay to duck and dodge and bend over to pick up extra balloons, but you are not allowed to take your feet off the ground. Once hit by a balloon, the player is out. Last one standing wins.

A group can play this game too, as long as there is an even number of players. Just expand the number of balloons and the number of players standing back to back.

You can also set up teams, and have them pace off and shoot at the other side. The team with the last member standing wins.

Balloon Long Jump

OF PLAYERS: **2** OR **more**

YOU NEED:
> balloons of various sizes
> string for tying
> chalk

Mark a starting line on the ground with chalk. Blow up several big round balloons. Place them on the ground, then run up to the starting line and jump over the balloons. Add another balloon after each successful jump. Each turn ends with a bang.

Balloon Archery

YOU NEED:
> balloons of various sizes
> chalk
> bucket

Set a bucket on the ground and walk 5 paces away. Blow up a balloon but don't tie it off. Try to shoot it into the bucket using its own jet power and listen to it whine through the air.

Balloon Relay

OF PLAYERS: **6** OR **more**

YOU NEED:
   a balloon for each team plus extras, just in case

Divide the group into two teams. Mark a course. Team members stand at one end. At the starting line, set a balloon on the ground in front of each team. Ready, set, go! The first racers squat over their balloon, squeeze it between their legs (no hands!) and run, as best they can, down to the other end. Then they return and pass the balloon with their legs to the next racer on their team. The first team whose racers get through the course wins. This game is hilarious.

Balloon Head

YOU NEED:
balloons
paper and pencil for recording scores

Players must bounce the balloon off their heads and see how many times they can hit it with their heads without using their hands. The one who hits the balloon the most times (no arms or shoulders allowed either), wins.

Song Rewriter

 # OF PLAYERS: 2 OR more

YOU NEED:

pen or pencil	*Optional*
paper	toilet paper tubes
CDs or tapes	tape
boombox	tissue paper or newspapers

There are lots of songs that everyone recognizes the melody to—like "Three Blind Mice" or "Row, Row, Row Your Boat" or "Happy Birthday." You can also change words to songs from commercials.

1. Use the melody of a song you know, but write your own words.

At first, change just a few words. Put in people's names, places, or other things you know. As this gets easier, start changing the words even more.

2. Pass out the words to all your friends, including the name of the tune you've borrowed.

3. People will instantly be able to sing along, because they know the tune and the beat.

Lip-sync Singer

OF PLAYERS: **2** OR **more**

YOU NEED:

tape, CD, or record
song sheets
costumes

Optional
toilet paper tubes
tape
tissue paper or
newspapers

Most great musicals tell their story through music.

1. Choose a musical that you enjoy, such as *The Lion King*, *Annie*, or *Beauty and the Beast*. Or, pick a song from a tape or CD that you want to pretend you're singing.

2. Listen to the recording a few times to get a feel for the music.

3. Figure out who will sing which parts.

4. Split up the parts and begin to practice.

5. Have everyone get costumes to fit their roles—wigs, masks, or makeup will add a lot of fun to the show.

6. Get ready to sing!

TIP:
To make a microphone, use a toilet paper or paper towel tube for the handle. Crumple up tissue paper or newspaper and tape it to one end of the mike.

Dance Daringly in Denmark

OF PLAYERS: **2** OR **more**

This game is a dynamic, grown-up version of "*A* My Name Is Alice," but bouncing a ball is optional (it makes for a much harder game).

One player starts by saying, "I'm taking a trip to Argentina [for example]. What will I do there?"

Player #2 must answer with a verb and another word beginning with the same letter as the name of the place.

"Act arrogant in Argentina," would be a possible answer.

Then player #2 proposes another location: "I'm taking a trip to Barcelona," for example.

Player #3 (if there is one, or player #1 if there's not) answers that he or she will "Bake beans in Barcelona," and then throws a C to the next player, who may "Charm chimps in China," and so on.

When a player fails to answer three times, with a reasonable period elapsing after each response, that player is ruled out of the game.

The winner is the last player left.

Where Am I?

OF PLAYERS: **2-30**

YOU NEED:
>   paper and pencil
>   a hat or a bowl

PREPARATION:

Write a place such as those listed opposite on pieces of scrap paper, and put them in a hat or a bowl.

Player #1 selects one of the scraps, but doesn't tell what it is. She will have to reveal the place she is in through pantomime. The act may be serious or comic or both.

You can play this game with just one other person, dividing the scraps of paper between you and acting them out one at a time. Or you can make it into team play, as you would in a game of Charades, but in this game you are not allowed to do "sounds like" or syllable play. You have to act out the activity without any signals or tricks.

1. in a submarine
2. on a roof
3. in a gold mine
4. on parade
5. in a jewelry store
6. in a bank
7. in a zoo
8. in a lighthouse
9. in a theater
10. on a train
11. in a cafe
12. in a museum
13. in a library
14. in a fire station
15. aboard ship
16. up an apple tree
17. in a kitchen
18. in court
19. in the hospital
20. on a picnic
21. in the desert
22. on a spaceship
23. in an aquarium
24. in a closet
25. in a shoe shop
26. in a taxi
27. in a canoe
28. on a mountaintop
29. on a plane
30. on a bus
31. in the jungle
32. at a football game
33. on a roller coaster
34. in a pet shop
35. in a gymnasium
36. in a garden
37. in church
38. at a final examination
39. in a fashion show
40. on an iceberg
41. at a switchboard
42. in an office
43. in a supermarket
44. on a farm
45. in a band
46. in a chorus line
47. in jail
48. on the moon
49. at the ballet
50. at an ice skating rink

In the Manner of the Word

While one player, say Tara, is out of the room, the others decide on an adverb that she will have to guess. The clues are acted out by the other players—silently.

Let's say that the adverb is "sweetly." When Tara comes back into the room, she asks Jean to do a dance step, for example, "in the manner of the word." Or she tells Jean to walk with a book on her head, or eat a chocolate, or read a magazine—whatever she wants to ask—"in the manner of the word."

When Jean has executed a dance step reeking with sweetness, Tara asks another player to do the same thing, or to perform a different action. There is no limit to the number of guesses Tara gets, and the game goes on until she discovers the adverb. Then Tara selects a new guesser, preferably the one whose act revealed the adverb, and the game goes on.

Be sure to pick adverbs that are easy to act out, like:

aggressively	cleverly
angrily	clumsily
anxiously	coolly
bitterly	cruelly
brilliantly	daintily
brutally	demurely
charmingly	desperately
childishly	eagerly

flirtatiously
gently
gingerly
gratefully
hatefully
heavily
hotly
hypnotically
impatiently
indifferently
jokingly
languorously
laughingly
lethargically
lightly
lovingly
masterfully
mischievously
murderously
nastily
obsequiously
powerfully
prettily
rambunctiously

roughly
rudely
sadly
shamefacedly
sharply
significantly
sleepily
sneakily
softly
stonily
teasingly
tenderly
timidly
toughly
tremblingly
uncomfortably
untidily
venomously
viciously
wickedly
wisely
wistfully
zestfully

Musical Bumps

OF PLAYERS: **6** OR **more**

This Musical Chairs type of game has no chairs, just music. The leader plays the piano—or a record or tape, or may just clap. The players move to the rhythm. When the leader stops the music, or stops clapping, everyone must sit on the floor. The last person to sit is OUT and must go to the sidelines with the leader.

For a "sit" to be considered "safe," the contestant's bottom must touch the floor.

Vary the type of music or rhythm so that some is loud, some soft, some fast, some with a jazz beat. Vary the length of each segment too, so that the players are totally unprepared for the moment the sound stops. Use a few very short segments; they make the game more exciting.

If the music is on tape or record, change the volume control suddenly. Many players will sit down at the change in dynamics, without realizing the music is still playing and the game still going on. These players are OUT.

When just two players are left, they will be busy watching each other and there may be one tie after another, as they both hit the floor at the same time. If this happens, ask them to close their eyes while they move to the music. You'll soon have a winner.

Sleepover Recipes

First your friends come over. They check out your new stuff. They play your games. And someone says, "What's there to eat around here?" You say, "I've got this brand new book," and they say, "But books taste lousy!" You roll your eyes and aim everyone into the kitchen before they eat your goldfish.

With the recipes here you can let loose your chocolate passion, make main meals in minutes, and create the ultimate in yumminess. If you want munchies that are like gourmet arts and crafts, you came to the right place.

A word to the wild: The original kitchen was a hole in the ground with a fire inside. The one in your house may have a microwave instead, but you can still get hurt. Don't forget that knives, stoves, and hot pans are dangerous. And as you know, fingers don't grow back.

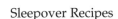

Classic Chocolate Chip Cookies

INGREDIENTS

- 1 egg
- 1 egg yolk
- 2¼ cups all purpose flour
- 1 teaspoon salt
- 1 teaspoon baking soda
- 12 tablespoons (1½ sticks) unsalted butter at room temperature
- ¾ cup light brown sugar
- ¾ cup granulated sugar
- 2½ teaspoons vanilla extract
- 1 package (12 ounces or 2 cups) semisweet chocolate chips

INSTRUCTIONS

1. Preheat oven to 350°F.

2. In a small bowl, whisk together one whole egg plus one egg yolk.

3. In a medium mixing bowl, sift together the flour, salt, and baking soda. Set aside.

4. Using an electric mixer, cream together the butter and both sugars until light and fluffy.

5. Add the eggs and vanilla extract into the butter and sugar mixture. Beat until smooth.

6. Slowly add the dry ingredients, mixing only until just blended.

7. With a wooden spoon, gently mix in the chocolate chips.

8. On a baking sheet, spoon tablespoon-size portions of the dough 3 inches apart.

9. Bake on the middle rack of the oven for 12–15 minutes.

10. Remove the baking sheet from the oven with potholders and cool the cookies on a wire rack for 5 minutes.

11. Repeat the process until all the cookies have been baked.

Makes 24 cookies.

TIP:
It's important not to overmix the dough after you add the dry ingredients or the cookies will be tough.

Banana Chocolate Drops

INGREDIENTS

> 1 package (12 ounces) semisweet chocolate chips
> 1 cup chopped peanuts
> 2 bananas, cut into 1-inch pieces

INSTRUCTIONS

1. In a small saucepan, bring 1 cup of water to a boil. Melt the chocolate chips by placing them in a stainless steel bowl and setting it on top of the saucepan.

2. Turn off the burner and allow the chocolate to melt over the steaming water.

3. While the chocolate is melting, select a baking sheet or large plate that fits into your freezer. Line it with wax paper or aluminum foil.

4. Place the peanuts in a small mixing bowl or on a plate. Set aside.

5. Stir the chocolate with a wooden spoon until it is smooth and completely melted.

6. Skewer each piece of banana with a toothpick and dip into the chocolate.

7. Roll the banana in the chocolate until completely coated.

8. Using the toothpick as a handle, roll the banana in the peanuts.

9. Place the coated banana on the baking sheet or plate.

10. Repeat the process until all banana pieces have been dipped.

11. Freeze bananas for 1 hour before serving.

Makes 10–12 drops.

TIP:
The peanuts stick better when the chocolate is still wet.

Fluffy S'Mores

INGREDIENTS

2 whole graham crackers
8 tablespoons marshmallow cream
1 bar (1½ ounces) plain chocolate, broken in half

INSTRUCTIONS

1. Break one whole graham cracker in half.

2. Spread 2 tablespoons of the marshmallow cream on each half.

3. Place half the chocolate bar between the two graham crackers.

4. Press the graham crackers together like a sandwich, with the chocolate in the center.

5. Repeat the process.

Makes 2 servings.

TIP:

Here are some variations:

- Substitute peanut butter for the marshmallow cream.
- Substitute bananas for the marshmallow cream.
- Substitute bananas for the chocolate.
- Substitute bananas and peanut butter for the chocolate and marshmallow cream.

Chicken Veggie Sticks

NOTE: You need 6 wooden or metal skewers for this recipe.

INGREDIENTS
    3 chicken breasts, boneless and skinless
    3 small zucchinis
    12 button mushrooms
    12 cherry tomatoes

INSTRUCTIONS
1. Preheat oven to 350°F.

2. Cut each chicken breast into 6 equal pieces.

3. Cut the zucchini into thick round slices.

4. On each skewer alternately place 3 pieces of chicken, 2 mushrooms, and 2 cherry tomatoes.

5. Repeat this process 5 times, until all the skewers have been filled.

6. Place kebabs on a baking sheet.

7. Bake on the middle rack of the oven for 15–20 minutes or until the chicken is white and soft.

8. Remove from the oven using potholders and serve while warm.

Makes 6 servings.

TIP: Tastes great served over white rice with soy sauce.

Rockin' Roll-Ups

INGREDIENTS

1 package (8 ounces) cream cheese at room temperature
1 tablespoon honey Dijon mustard
1 cup (2 sticks) unsalted butter
8 slices white bread
¾ pound thinly sliced ham
1 cup grated Parmesan cheese
Vegetable cooking spray

INSTRUCTIONS

1. Preheat oven to 300°F.

2. In a small mixing bowl, combine the cream cheese with the mustard.

3. Melt the butter in the microwave or in a small saucepan on the stone. Transfer the melted butter to a small mixing bowl.

4. Slice the crusts off the bread.

5. Using a rolling pin, roll each piece of bread very thin.

6. Spread the cream cheese mixture evenly on each slice of bread.

7. Place a thin slice of ham on each piece of bread and roll up lengthwise.

8. Dip the roll into melted butter.

9. Sprinkle the roll with Parmesan cheese.

10. Place the rolls 1 inch (2.5 cm) apart on a lightly sprayed baking sheet.

11. Bake on the middle rack of the oven for 10–15 minutes or until lightly golden.

12. Remove from the oven with potholders and let cool slightly before serving.

Makes 8 servings.

TIP:
For a vegetarian variation, substitute 1 teaspoon of lemon pepper for the Dijon mustard and asparagus spears for the ham.

Peanut Butter and Jelly Cake

INGREDIENTS

1 store-bought pound cake
½ cup of your favorite fruit jelly

For the frosting
¼ cup creamy peanut butter
3 tablespoons unsalted butter or margarine at room
   temperature
1 teaspoon vanilla extract
2 cups powdered sugar, sifted
¼ cup milk

INSTRUCTIONS

1. Cut the pound cake in half down the middle.

2. Spread the jelly evenly on the cut sides of the cake.

3. Sandwich the two sides back together. Set aside.

4. Using an electric mixer, cream together the butter and the peanut butter until they are light and fluffy.

5. Add the vanilla and continue beating.

6. Add the sugar and milk, a little at a time, and continue beating until smooth and spreadable.

7. Cover the entire cake with the peanut butter frosting.

Makes 8–10 servings.

TIP:
To measure the peanut butter, fill a measuring cup with ¾ cup of water, then put in enough peanut butter to bring the water level to the top of the cup. Pour out the water.

It is easier to mix the frosting when the butter and peanut butter are at room temperature.

Dirt Pies

Even better tasting than s'mores, these delicious pies are eaten with a fork, and are great with milk.

INGREDIENTS

   2 cups chocolate cookie crumbs
      (about 30 cookies with the cream filling removed)
   ¼ cup sugar
   ¼ teaspoon salt
   1 stick (½ cup) unsalted butter, melted
   6 (about 1½ ounces each) milk chocolate bars
   3½ cups mini-marshmallows

INSTRUCTIONS

1. Preheat oven to 350°F.

2. To make the cookie crumbs, peel apart the cookies and scrape out the middle. Put the outside portions inside a resealable plastic bag and seal. Run a rolling pin over the bag until the cookies are crushed into crumbs.

3. Melt the butter over low heat.

4. Put the melted butter, crumbs, sugar, and salt into a large bowl. Mix well.

5. Press the mixture into the bottom and sides of six small disposable aluminum bowls.

6. Place the bowls on cookie sheets and bake for 10 minutes.

7. Using potholders, take the crusts out of the oven and set aside to cool on wire racks.

8. Increase the oven temperature to 450°F.

9. Melt the chocolate bars in a metal bowl set over a saucepan of barely simmering water. Keep stirring the chocolate until smooth.

10. Pour the chocolate evenly into the six crusts.

11. Top each pie with marshmallows, pressing them lightly into the chocolate.

12. Put the cookie sheets with the pans of dirt pies into the preheated oven for about 2 minutes, or until the marshmallows are golden.

13. Remove from the oven with potholders and cool briefly before serving. (That means cool it and wait a few minutes.)

Dirt never tasted so good!

Basket-of-Berries Smoothies

INGREDIENTS

1 cup of milk, nonfat or lowfat
½ cup nonfat frozen yogurt or fruit sherbet
1 banana
½ cup of fresh or frozen berries

INSTRUCTIONS

1. Put ingredients in a blender, one at a time.

2. Blend all ingredients until smooth.

3. Serve in chilled glasses.

Makes 1–2 servings.

TIPS:

Use any kind of berries or a combination.
For a healthier drink, substitute soy milk for the regular milk.

Math Magic and Tricks

2 5 8 % = + 1 7

So you think math is boring—essential probably, but deadly and dreary, and for people who want to be accountants. Well, you probably think that because you haven't learned the sneaky, sly, spectacular tricks that you can play—using math!

Here you'll find all sorts of ways to baffle, confuse, and deceive your friends and family, and anyone else you meet, with numbers. There's no sleight of hand, no hidden moves to worry about. These tricks work automatically! All you need is paper and pencil, and a captive audience!

Go ahead—dare to be amazing!

Three-Digit Miracle

You can use this very intriguing maneuver as the basis for many other tricks.

Take any 3-digit number: **197**, for example.
Write it backwards:	**791**
Subtract the smaller number:	**197**
Total:	**594**
Now write **594** backwards:	**495**
Add it to the previous total.	**1089**

What's so miraculous about that? No matter what 3-digit number you use, you'll always come up with 1089!

NOTE:
If you get the number 99 as the "total" number, look out. Remember, it isn't 99 at all, but 099. So when you write it backwards, write 990.
Example: **211** is the number you pick:
Write it backwards:	**211**
Subtract the smaller number:	**112**
Total:	**099**
Write it backwards:	**990**
Add it to the previous total.	**1089**

The only numbers that won't work are numbers that are written the same backwards and forwards, such as 141, 252, 343, and so on.

Who's Got the String?

YOU NEED:
a piece of string

Number all the players in the group and ask them to tie a string on someone's finger while you leave the room or turn your back. Offer to tell them not only who has it, but which hand and which finger it is placed on!

But first, ask one of the players to make the following calculations for you:

1. Multiply the number of the person with the string by 2.
2. Add 3.
3. Multiply the result by 5.
4. Add 8 if the string is on the right hand.
   Add 9 if the string is on the left hand.
5. Multiply by 10.
6. Add the number of the finger (the thumb is 1).
7. Add 2.

When you are told the resulting number, mentally subtract 222. The remainder gives the answer, beginning with the right-hand digit.

For example, suppose the string is on the left hand, third finger of Player #4.

Player's number (4) multiplied by 2	**8**
Add 3	**11**
Multiply by 5	**55**
Add 9 (for left hand)	**64**
Multiply by 10	**640**
Add finger number (3)	**643**
Add 2	**645**
Subtract 222	**423**

The right-hand digit stands for the finger—the third finger. The middle digit stands for the hand (1 would be the right hand), and the first digit is the number of the person.

When the number of the person is above 9, the two left-hand digits indicate the number of the person.

The Secret Number

People who are good at math won't have much trouble figuring out why this trick works. Others will be mystified completely. Tell your friends that you are going to read the numbers in their minds, if they do what you tell them to.

Ask them to think of a number, but not to tell it to you. Then ask them to:

1. Double that number (mentally).
2. Multiply by 5, and tell you the result.

You knock off the zero on the end, and the remainder is the secret number.

For example, your friend may take 7. Doubling it makes it 14, and multiplying it by 5 makes 70. Knock off the zero, and 7 is your answer. It always works because doubling the number and then multiplying it by 5 is just the same as multiplying it by 10. When you take off the zero, of course, you have the original number.

If this is too simple for your audience, tell them that you will guess two numbers at a time. Tell them to think of two numbers from 1 to 9, but not to tell you what they are. Tell them now to:

1. Multiply either number by 5.
2. Then add 7
3. And double the sum.
4. Then add the other original secret number
5. And subtract 14.

When they tell you the result, it will be a 2-digit number and each digit will be one of the secret numbers.

For example, if someone thought of 2 and 9, and took 9 first, it would go like this:

$$9 \times 5 = 45$$
$$\underline{+7}$$
$$52$$

$$52 \times 2 = 104$$
$$\underline{+2}$$
$$106$$

$$106 - 14 = 92$$

Just as in the first example, you are asking your friends to multiply the original number by 5 and then 2, or by 10 all together. The 7 is merely to confuse them, for after doubling it, you tell them to subtract the doubled 7 by taking off 14. When they add the second number to 10 times the first one, you naturally get the two secret numbers.

Math Magic

With this fascinating trick, you can add large numbers with remarkable speed and accuracy.

Ask your audience to write down 2 rows of figures, each containing 5 digits, such as:

1st row: **3 4 6 5 8**
2nd row: **4 6 8 2 9**

Now you put down a third row of figures:

3rd row: **5 3 1 7 0**

Ask your audience to put down a fourth:

4th row: **6 2 3 5 3**

Now you write a fifth row:

5th row: **3 7 6 4 6**

Then you look at the figures a moment and write on a small piece of paper, fold the paper, and give it to someone in the audience to hold. Then ask the audience to add up the numbers and call out the total. When they figure it out, call for your slip of paper and unfold it. There—for everyone to see—is the correct total!

How it is done: You work your calculations while you are putting down your rows of figures. When you write the third row, make each of your numbers total 9 when added to the number just above it in the second row. (Ignore the top row.) In the fifth row, make each number total 9 when added to the number in the fourth row.

Now you can figure out the grand total very quickly by using the first line. Just subtract 2 from the last number of the first line (in this case, the number is an 8), and place the 2 in front of the first number, so it goes like this:

Audience:	**3**	**4**	**6**	**5**	**8**
Audience:	**4**	**6**	**8**	**2**	**9**
You:	**5**	**3**	**1**	**7**	**0**
Audience:	**6**	**2**	**3**	**5**	**3**
You:	**3**	**7**	**6**	**4**	**6**
	2 3	**4**	**6**	**5**	**6**

Exceptions: If the audience writes a first number that ends in either 0 or 1, you need to mentally reverse the first and second rows of figures. When you write the third row, put down numbers that total 9 when added to the numbers in the first row. Ignore the second row until the grand total. Follow the same procedure as usual with the fourth and fifth rows. But figure the grand total by using the second line— subtracting 2 from the last number and placing 2 in front of the first number, like this:

Audience:	**3**	**4**	**6**	**5**	**0**
Audience:	**4**	**6**	**9**	**2**	**9**
You:	**6**	**5**	**3**	**4**	**9**
Audience:	**6**	**2**	**3**	**5**	**3**
You:	**3**	**7**	**6**	**4**	**6**
	2 4	**6**	**9**	**2**	**7**

Magic Number

YOU NEED:

> paper and a pencil for you and everybody
> in your audience

There is actually a magic number that you can multiply with lightning speed in your head. The number is 142,857. Prepare yourself with paper and pencil and show your friends that the paper is blank. You will use it only to write down the result.

Now give your friends pencil and paper and ask them to multiply 142,857 by any number from 1 to 7. Then ask them, one at a time, to tell you any one figure in the result. Suppose the third figure from the left is 5. You know immediately that the entire total is 285,714! You also know that the multiplier was 2.

Suppose the fourth figure from the left is 4: then you know the total is 571,428 and the multiplier is 4.

Do you get it? Every possible total of this magic number, when multiplied by 1 to 6, results in the same series of digits, but it begins at a different point. Multiply them out if you want to check, or run them through a calculator. Therefore, if you know the position of any one number in the sequence, you are able to write down the total correctly. In the example above, when your friend told you that 4 was the fourth figure, you put down 428 at the end of the total and 571 in the front, according to the sequence.

How do you know what the number was multiplied by? Look at the last digit you wrote down. Since 4 x 7 = 28 (and this is the only combination that ends in an 8), the multiplier gives itself away. That last digit is different for each multiplication.

By the way, if you multiply the magic number by 7, you get another magic number:

999,999

Number Wizard

You are the number wizard. Ask your friends to choose any number from 1 to 10 without telling you what it is. Then tell them to add 8 to it in their heads (keeping it secret), double it, divide it by 4, and then subtract half of the original number. So it goes like this:

Their number:	**8**
Add 8:	**16**
Double it:	**32**
Divide by 4:	**8**
Subtract half the original number:	**−4**
Answer:	**4**

"The answer is 4," you say, and you are right! Even though your friends haven't told you a thing about their numbers.

If you had told them to add 6 to the original number, the answer would be 3.

How does it work? The remainder is always half the number you tell them to add. Everything else cancels out.

Or try this one:

"Take a number," you say. "Add 7, double it, add 16, double it again, divide by 4, and subtract 15. Now you each have the number you started with!"

Mystifying? Still, it's simple to figure out, because the doubling, dividing, adding, and subtracting cancel out, and you have really done nothing to change the original number.

5

Brain Bafflers

Lateral thinking puzzles, logic puzzles, math puzzles—the mind-benders in this section have lots of variety. They're all interesting, tricky, and short. They set up the situation fast, and you can solve them mentally in just a minute or two. Test yourself, or your family and friends, or play them at a party like a TV quiz show. But look out—the answers are not always obvious, and sometimes you may be misled. So use your imagination, stay alert, and have an open mind when you figure out your answers.

Solutions are at the back of the book.

1. Emily is taller than Ann and shorter than Dolores. Who is the tallest of the three?

2. A woman has five children and half of them are male. Is this possible?

3. There are 100 buildings along a street. A sign maker is ordered to number the buildings from 1 to 100. How many 9s will be needed?

4. How many tickets with different points of origination and destination can be sold on a bus line that travels a loop of 25 stops?

5. We know that humans have up to 100,000 hairs. In a city with more than 200,000 people, would it be possible to find two or more people with the same number of hairs?

6. All Lisa's scarves are red except two. All her scarves are blue except two. All her scarves are green except two. How many scarves does she have?

7. Which is warmer: a two-inch thick blanket or two blankets, each one inch thick?

8. A street that's 30 yards (30 m) long has a chestnut tree every 6 yards (6 m) on both sides. How many chestnut trees are on the entire street?

9. Jennifer and Amy had a picnic. Jennifer had already eaten half of the muffins when Amy ate half the remaining muffins plus three more. There were no muffins left. How many muffins did they bring to the picnic?

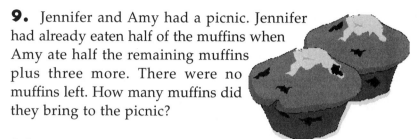

10. A little town has two hair salons. The first one has a dirty mirror and a floor covered with hair, and the hairdresser has an awful haircut. In the second one, the mirror and floor are very clean, and the hairdresser has a great haircut. Where would you go and why?

11. In the fifth century A.D., a king was taking his daily bath when he received a huge crown that he had ordered made from one of his bars of gold. He knew that the crown and the gold weighed the same, although he suspected that part of the gold had been replaced with lighter materials, such as copper or silver. How did he find out quickly?

12. A medieval count organized a court trial in which he gave the defendant a chance to save his life if he could pick a white marble out of a bag containing, in the count's words, "one white marble and one black marble." The accused knew that this was a trick because he had seen the count place two black marbles in the bag. However, he went ahead and took out a marble. What did he do to save his life?

13. If we tie a light oxygen tank to a bird so that it can breathe on the moon, would the bird fly faster, slower, or at the same speed as it does on earth? (Remember that there is less gravity on the moon.)

14. One mother gave 25 books to her daughter and another mother gave her daughter 8 books. However, between both daughters they increased their collection by only 25 books. How can this be?

15. When Ellen went to visit her friend Albert, she found him dead at his desk with a bullet through his head. She saw a cassette player and decided to listen to the tape. She hit "Play" and heard, "This is Albert. I just got a call saying that someone is on his way here to kill me and he will be here in less than three minutes. I hear steps. Someone is opening the door." At that point, Ellen knew that it was not Albert's voice on the tape, but the killer's. How did she know?

16. Samantha was working in her home office when she realized that she had left a hundred-dollar bill in the book she had been reading. She called her butler to bring her the book from the library. When she got it, the bill was no longer there. She then questioned the maid and the butler. The maid remembered seeing the bill between pages 99 and 100 in a book to the left of a business book. The butler did not recall seeing the bill, but was sure the book was to the right of the business book, because to the left of it was a book on statistics. Who is lying?

17. Every day, a cyclist crosses the border between Spain and France carrying a bag. No matter how many times customs officials investigate her, they do not know what she is smuggling. Do you?

18. A sultan wanted to offer his daughter in marriage to the candidate whose horse would win a certain race. However, the rules of the race stated that the winner would be the one in last place. He didn't want the race to last forever, so he thought of a way to solve this problem. What was it?

19. My cousin Diana was once kidnapped. She knew they would either take her to New York or to Sydney, Australia. When they took her blindfold off, she could see that she had been locked in a room without windows. There was only a table, a bed, a chair, and a sink. However, Diana was able to figure out which city she was in. How did she do it?

20. These are the clues to a robbery and murder in a ground floor office:
A. The killer had to be one of three people: the muscular engineer, the obese director, or the perky secretary.
B. The stolen goods were taken out through the open window. There were light footprints under it in the snow.
C. The footprints matched the director's shoes, which were found next to the crime weapon.
D. Only one bullet was found, although there were two wounds to the body: one to the chest and the other to the right hand.
   Who was the killer? Why were there two wounds?

21. Holly just made herself a cup of coffee and has realized she must run upstairs for a minute. She doesn't want the coffee to get cold, and she has to add milk at room temperature. Should she add the milk before she goes upstairs or when she gets back?

22. A spider spins its web in a window frame. Each day it spins an area equal to that of the amount already completed. It takes this spider 30 days to cover the entire window frame. How long would two spiders take if each of them spins an amount equal to the area of the existing part of the web made by that particular spider?

23. Dan was used to walking at a regular pace. He never wore a watch, although he had a very accurate clock at home. One day, he forgot to wind it, and the clock stopped. He went to Lee's house two miles away to ask the time. He spent the afternoon and when he came back home, he set the clock to the exact time. How did he know what that was?

24. If 75% of all women are tall, 75% are brunette, and 75% are brown-eyed, what is the minimum percentage of tall, brunette, brown-eyed women?

25. We have two similar coins and we make one spin on the edge of the other. How many times does the spinning coin turn on itself each time it makes an entire lap around the stationary one?

6

Beautiful Beads

With even the simplest patterns, you can use beads to make amazing jewelry.

Start by visiting a bead store. Explore. Look at all the amazing colors, shapes, and sizes of beads. Hold them in your hands to see how they feel. Imagine what you are going to say with the beads.

Beads come in a huge variety. The ones in this section are mostly small glass or plastic beads, and they are measured in millimeters (mm). There are 25 mm to an inch.

The smallest beads are called seed beads. Their size is 11/0 (also written 11°). It takes about 16 seed beads to fill an inch.

A larger size of bead is called the e bead, size 6/0 (or 6°). You get about 6 to the inch.

Bugle beads are tubular glass or plastic beads that are measured by their length.

THREADS

For some patterns, the thread has to go through a bead more than once. Use strong, thin thread with a thickness of 5 mm or less. Clear nylon monofilament thread is also good, as is very thin wire, such as 26-gauge. The higher the gauge, the thinner the wire. If you use wire, you won't need a needle.

CLASPS

Many different kinds of clasps are available. Barrel clasps, which look like little barrels and screw together, are good for necklaces and anklets, but not for bracelets because they're hard to put on with one hand.

MAKING KNOTS

When you start or finish a bead project using thread, you'll have to make a knot. Double overhand knots are the easiest:

1. An overhand knot is made like a loop with a thread through it.

2. To make a double knot, pass the thread through a loop like an overhand knot and then repeat that step.

3. To attach a clasp, use a double overhand knot like this:

4. If you're making a necklace with two strands, you can use a multiple-strand knot, like this.

Beware—knots can come undone. You can protect your knots by dabbing a little clear, washable glue on them with a toothpick. Clear nail polish also works.

NEATENING ENDS:
Leave a tail of 2 to 3" (5 to 7 cm) before tying on your thread. When you finish beading, put the thread tail through a needle and run it back through a few beads. Tie it a few times between two of the beads and then clip off the extra thread tail.

If you use wire, twist a tail of about 1" (2.5 cm) around the main wire 4 or 5 times before you start beading.

Finish the project in the same way. Trim off the excess wire end and make sure it isn't sticking out so it doesn't poke anyone.

Simply Beads Necklace

YOU NEED:
>clear seed beads
>black seed beads
>light purple bugle beads length ½" (13 mm)
>thread
>clasp
>needle (optional)

1. Tie a 23" (58 cm) thread to one end of a clasp, leaving a 3" (7.5 cm) tail and making a double knot (two overhand knots) with the short end of the thread

2. String one clear seed bead.

3. String one black seed bead.

4. Add a clear seed bead.

5. Add a purple bugle bead.

6. Again, string one clear, one black, one clear seed bead, and then a purple bugle bead.

7. Continue this pattern until you get a length that fits comfortably around your neck.

8. Finish by tying on the second end of the clasp with a double knot and neatening the ends.

Floating Beads Necklace

YOU NEED:
> any beads you like
> clear thread (plastic or nylon)
> clasp

1. Tie an 18" (46 cm) thread to a clasp 1½" (3.8 cm) from the end.

2. Make a double knot about 1" (2.5 cm) in from the clasp. You may have to make more knots, depending on the size of the bead hole, to hold the bead in place. Pull the knot tight.

3. Add a bead.

4. Make another knot right after the bead.

5. Pull the knot tight.

6. Make another knot 1" (2.5 cm) from the last knot.

7. Add a bead and make another knot after it.

8. Continue adding three more beads the same way.

Make sure the necklace is a good length to fit around your neck. Finish by attaching the thread end to the second half of the clasp.

Waves and Pearls Anklet

YOU NEED:
>   pearls
>   purple e beads
>   thread
>   clasp

1. Center one end of a clasp on a 24" (61 cm) thread. Secure the clasp with a double knot. String one purple e bead onto both thread ends. Separate the threads and add a pearl to the top thread.

2. Add 4 purple e beads to the bottom strand.

3. Put both threads together and add on a purple e bead.

4. Push the beads close together so there is no space between them.

5. Add 4 purple e beads to the top thread. Add one pearl to the bottom thread.

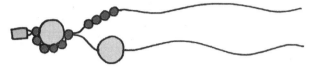

6. Put both threads together and add one purple e bead.

7. Again, pull really hard so there is no extra space and the beads are right up against each other.

8. Add one pearl on the top thread and 4 purple e beads on the bottom thread.

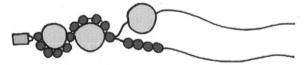

9. Add one purple e bead on both threads together.

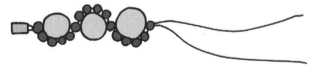

10. Continue this pattern until the length fits around your ankle. Tie the threads to the other end of the clasp. Neaten the ends.

Roman Headband

YOU NEED:
>black e beads
>clear e beads
>elastic thread 1 mm thick

1. Tie two pieces of 18" (46 cm) elastic thread together, 2" (5 cm) from the ends.

2. String beads on one thread, alternating 2 black e beads and 2 clear e beads. Keep adding beads until you get a length that fits snugly around your head. Check to make sure that the headband fits well; take away or add beads as needed.

3. String beads on the second thread in the same way, making the second strand the same length as the first one.

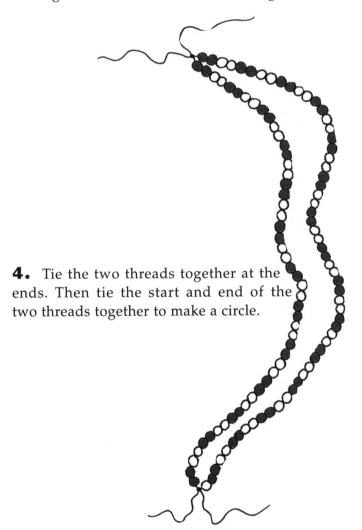

4. Tie the two threads together at the ends. Then tie the start and end of the two threads together to make a circle.

When you wear the headband, separate the two strands, leaving a space in between to wear it like a Roman headband. Push the strands together for a different look.

Star in Your Hair

YOU NEED:

- silver ½" (13 mm) bugle beads
- purple seed beads
- wire (24 gauge)
- bobby pin (hairpin)

1. On a wire that is 18" long (46 cm), string one purple seed bead and one silver bugle bead.

2. Continue stringing one purple seed bead and then one silver bugle bead until you have a total of 10 seed beeds and 8 bugle beads.

3. Push the beads close together so there is no extra space between them and at least 1" (2.5 cm) of empty wire at the start and at the end. Bend the wire as shown to make a star point.

4. Repeat until you get the shape of a star.

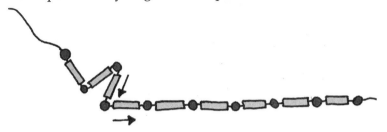

5. Twist the two ends of the wire together after making 5 points.

6. Use the extra wire to twist around the bobby pin to attach the star.

Crossing Strands Bracelet

YOU NEED:

> red seed beads
> brown seed beads
> thread
> clasp

1. Center one end of a clasp on a 22" (56 cm) thread. Secure the clasp with a double knot. String one brown bead on both threads.

2. Separate the threads and add 11 brown beads to one of them.

3. Add 11 red seed beads to the other thread.

4. Put the threads together and string one brown bead.

5. Add 11 brown beads to the bottom thread.

6. Add 11 red beads to the top thread.

7. Put the threads together and string a brown bead.

8. Continue the pattern until you get a length that fits around your wrist. Finish by attaching the thread ends to the other side of the clasp. Neaten the ends.

Squares Bracelet

YOU NEED:
> blue bugle beads, ½" (13 mm)
> silver bugle beads, ½" (13 mm)
> thread
> clasp

1. Center one end of a clasp on a 22" (56 cm) thread. Secure the clasp with a double knot. Add a blue bugle bead to one of the two threads.

2. String the other thread through the same blue bugle bead in the opposite direction.

3. Add a silver bugle bead to each of the two threads.

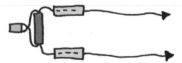

4. String another blue bugle bead on one thread.

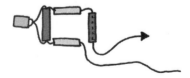

5. String the other thread through the same blue bugle bead in the opposite direction.

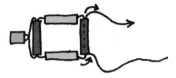

6. Pull tight to make sure there is no extra space between beads.

7. Continue the pattern until you get a length that fits around your wrist.

8. Finish by attaching the other end of the clasp. Neaten up the ends.

Squares Headband

YOU NEED:

> bugle beads, as for the Squares Bracelet
> elastic thread

Follow the same instructions as for the Squares Bracelet, but use elastic thread, and make sure the strand will be long enough to fit around your head.

Quick Science Experiments

Here are over a dozen fascinating science experiments you can do easily in minutes using ordinary things you have around the house. They range from tricks with light to magical properties that you can give to balloons, liquids, and plants, to strange manipulations that no one will be able to explain, such as how you can suspend an egg in the middle of a jar.

You'll find experiments with sound, plus optical illusions—and other kinds of illusions too, like the experience of having two noses! You'll even discover how to charm a paper snake!

All the experiments are short, quick, and fun. You'll love sharing them with friends, family, and classmates.

Light Fan

YOU NEED:
    a light-colored rod

Hold a light-colored rod between your thumb and forefinger and move it quickly up and down in neon light. You do not see, as you might expect, a single blurred, bright line, but what appears to resemble an oriental fan with light and dark ribs.

    Neon tubes contain a gas, which flashes on and off 60 times a second (in the U.S.) because of rapid reversals in alternating current. The moving rod is thrown alternately into light and darkness in rapid sequence, so that it seems to move by jerks in a semicircle. The light from a television set will produce the same effect. Normally, the eye is too slow to notice these breaks in illumination clearly. In a regular electric light bulb, the metal filament continues glowing between the peaks in current.

Clinging Balloons

YOU NEED:
> balloons
> string for tying them
> wool sweater

Blow up some balloons and rub them for a short time on a wool sweater. If you place them against the ceiling, they will remain there for hours.

The balloons become negatively charged with static electricity when they are rubbed; that is, they remove minute, negatively charged particles, called electrons, from the sweater. Because electrically charged bodies are weakly attracted to those that are neutral, or uncharged, the balloons cling to the ceiling until the charges between the two gradually become equal. This generally takes hours in a dry atmosphere, because the electrons flow slowly from the balloons into the ceiling, which is a poor conductor.

Hostile Balloons

YOU NEED:
> balloons
> string for tying them and joining them
> wool sweater

Blow up two balloons and join them with string. Rub both on a wool sweater and let them hang downwards from the string. Instead of being attracted, like the balloons were to the ceiling, they float away from each other.

When rubbed, both balloons become negatively charged because they have taken electrons from the sweater, which has now gained a positive charge. Negative and positive charges attract each other, so the balloons will stick to the sweater. Similar charges, however, repel—so the balloons move away from each other.

String of Pearls

YOU NEED:
 a basin or sink with running water

Hold your finger under the tap and let a fine jet of water pour over it. If you look carefully, you will see a strange wavelike pattern in the water above your finger. If you bring your finger closer to the tap, the waves become increasingly ball-shaped, until the water jet resembles a string of pearls. The flow is so strongly obstructed by your finger that because of its surface tension—the force that holds the water molecules together—it backs up and forms round droplets. If you take your finger farther away from the tap, the falling speed of the water becomes greater, and the drop formation is less clear.

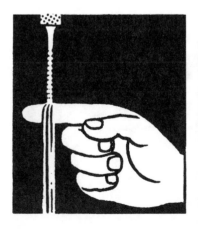
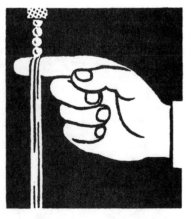

Water Lily

YOU NEED:
> writing paper
> crayons
> water

Cut out a flower shape from smooth writing paper, color it with crayons, and fold the petals firmly inward. If you place the paper flower on water, you will see the petals open in slow motion.

Paper consists mainly of plant fibers, which are composed of extremely fine tubes. The water fills these so-called capillary tubes, causing the paper to swell and the petals of the flower to open up, like the leaves of a wilting plant when it is placed in water.

The Suspended Egg

YOU NEED:
> a jar
> water
> salt
> egg

Fill a jar halfway with water and dissolve plenty of salt in it. Now add the same amount of water again, pouring carefully over a spoon so that the two liquids do not mix. An egg placed in the jar remains suspended in the middle.

Since the egg is heavier than tap water, but lighter than salt water, it sinks only to the middle of the jar and floats on the salt water. You can use a raw potato instead of an egg. Cut a roundish "magic fish" from it, and make fins and eyes from colored cellophane.

Egg Detection

YOU NEED:
> eggs: one hard-boiled, one uncooked
> plate

There is a very simple method for distinguishing a hard-boiled egg from a raw one without breaking the shell. Spin the eggs on a plate, and the cooked one will continue to rotate. Since its center of gravity lies in the thicker half, it even stays upright, like a top.

The liquid inside the raw egg prevents this. Since the yolk is heavier than the white, it rolls from the middle when you spin the egg, because of centrifugal force. It brakes the movement so much that it only amounts to a clumsy rocking.

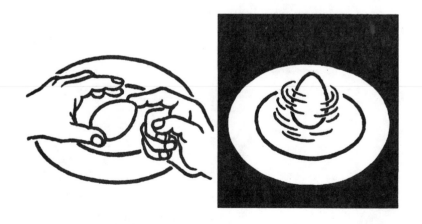

Water Organ

YOU NEED:
    a thin-walled glass with water

Half fill a thin-walled glass with water, dip in your forefinger, and run it slowly around the rim of the glass. With a little practice, you will produce a lovely continuous ringing sound.

    This experiment works best if you have just washed your finger. It rubs over the glass, giving it tiny jolts. The glass begins to vibrate, which is what produces the note. (You can clearly see the vibration on the surface of the water.) If your finger is greasy, it slides smoothly over the glass without the necessary friction. The pitch of the note depends on the amount of water in the glass.

The Magic Rabbit

YOU NEED:
    this page

Look at this picture at the normal reading distance. Then shut your left eye and stare at the magic rod with your right eye. Now slowly alter the distance of the picture from your eyes—abracadabra! The rabbit suddenly disappears!

The retina of the eye consists of a large number of light-sensitive nerve endings called rods and cones. There is one spot, however, where there are no rods or cones to detect light. It is located where the nerves join together to form the optic nerve. If the image of the rabbit thrown on the retina falls at this "blind spot" as you move the picture, you cannot see it.

Moon Rocket

YOU NEED:
   this page

Hold the picture so that the tip of your nose touches the star, and turn it around slowly to the left. The rocket flies into the sky and lands again on the moon. Each eye receives its own image, and both impressions are transmitted to the brain, which combines them. If you hold the star to the tip of your nose, your right eye sees only the rocket and your left eye only the moon. As usual, the halves of the image are combined in the brain. As you turn the picture on its edge and squint, it does not shrink anymore because both eyes see the same image.

Two Noses

YOU NEED:
> no special equipment

Cross your index and middle fingers and rub them sideways over the tip of your nose. To your great surprise, you will feel two noses.

When you cross them over, the position of the sides of the fingers is switched. The sides normally facing away from one another are now next to each other, and both touch the tip of your nose at the same time. Each one reports separately to your brain, as usual, about its contact with your nose. This is deceiving because the brain does not realize that you have crossed your fingers.

Ghostly Noise

YOU NEED:
> a small water glass
> dried peas
> metal lid

Fill a small water glass to overflowing with dried peas. Pour in water up to the brim, and place the glass on a metal lid. The heap of peas becomes slowly higher and then a clatter of falling peas begins, which goes on for hours!

This is a process of osmosis. Water penetrates the pea cells through the skin and dissolves the nutrients in them. The pressure thus formed makes the peas swell. In the same way, the water necessary for life penetrates the walls of all plant cells, stretching them. If the plant obtains insufficient water, its cells become flabby and it wilts.

The Coiled Snake

YOU NEED:
>   thin tissue paper
>   scissors
>   metal lid
>   fountain pen

Cut a spiral-shaped coil from a thin piece of tissue paper about 4 inches (10 cm) square, lay it on a tin lid, and bend its head up. Rub a fountain pen vigorously with a wool cloth and hold it over the coil. It will rise like a living snake and reach upward.

In this case, the fountain pen has taken electrons from the woolen cloth and attracts the uncharged paper. On contact, the paper falls because it takes part of the negative electric charge and gives it up immediately to the metal lid, which is a good conductor. Since the paper is now uncharged again, it is once more attracted upward until the fountain pen loses its charge.

Where Is the Wind Coming From?

YOU NEED:
> no special equipment

Moisten your finger and hold it straight up in the air. You will notice at once that one side of your finger is cold. This is the direction from which the wind is coming.

Heat is used up when a liquid vaporizes or evaporates. The wind accelerates the evaporation of the moisture on the finger, and you will notice, even with a weak air current, the greater heat loss on the side facing the wind. Anybody who keeps on a wet bathing suit after a swim will shiver even on a warm day. The water takes heat from the body as it evaporates.

Wind ▶

Nature in a Bottle

YOU NEED:

>an airtight, clear glass bottle or jar, with top
>small pebbles
>charcoal scraps
>funnel (optional)
>soil
>peat
>½ teaspoon of bone meal
>water
>ferns and mosses

Plants can live for a long time without attention in an airtight, clear glass bottle or jar. First insert small pebbles and pieces of charcoal, using a funnel if necessary. Next add some soil mixed with peat and half a teaspoonful of bone meal. Add enough water to make the soil damp but not soggy. Choose only slow-growing, nonflowering plants, such as small ferns and mosses. With the aid of some wire instruments, place them on the damp soil.

Close the bottle firmly and keep it in a light place, but away from direct sunlight. Open the bottle only occasionally to remove dry leaves and perhaps to add a little water.

In the "bottle garden," the food cycle functions almost exactly as in the open air:

1) The plants absorb water from the soil and evaporate most of it through their leaves. The moisture condenses in droplets on the glass walls and falls like rain to the ground.

2) The plants breathe in carbon dioxide and breathe out oxygen (the opposite of what we do). Some of the oxygen is absorbed again during the hours of darkness. The rest is absorbed by bacteria in the soil and by fungi which, in turn, produce carbon dioxide.

3) The plants need light to power the green chlorophyll molecules in the leaves, which manufacture starch (the plant's main food) from water and carbon dioxide. The starch is broken down into its original components, as parts of the plant decay.

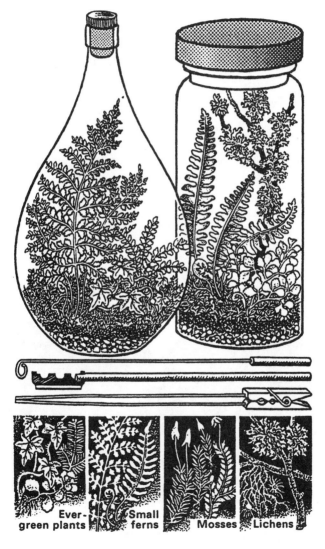

Ever-green plants   Small ferns   Mosses   Lichens

Seeing Inside an Orange

Before peeling an orange, you can tell someone how many slices it contains. This trick is accomplished by removing from an orange the small green or brown part of the plant that once formed at the bottom of the orange blossom. Within the hole left behind is a circle of small dots. Each one indicates one orange slice; a very small one hints at a thin slice.

The dots are the remains of the seed vessels in the orange blossom, which are arranged in a circle. After being pollinated, the seed vessels develop into the orange slices, which form the fruit.

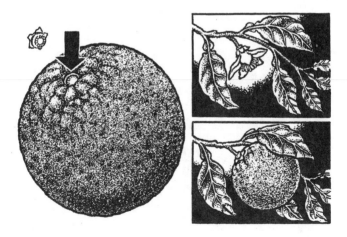

Fortune-
Telling Games

8

How many ways are there to tell fortunes? Literally thousands, maybe tens of thousands! People have been trying to find out what life has in store for them ever since they were able to think about the future. Would they be safe? Would they have enough to eat? Would the people they love love them back?

And because people want to know the answers so intensely, they'll try anything to find out, with anything they have at hand. Got a buttercup? Put it under your chin. If your chin shines yellow, you're in love. A coin? Flip it. Heads you do/will/are, tails you don't/won't/aren't.

Is there anything to it? Do any of these techniques work? According to the psychics and the seers, they all work. Your inner self knows the answer to every question. When you're ready to pick up the information, it provides it willingly through whatever means you allow. So any system can work, even one you make up yourself for fun.

That's what they tell us. Here's a great assortment of easy, quick fortune-telling games—just for having fun. Believe them or not!

Will I Get My Wish?

OF PLAYERS: 1 OR more

YOU NEED:
> a deck of cards

For a quick yes or no answer to a question, take an ordinary deck of cards and pull out every card under the rank of 7. Use only the higher value cards, 7s through Aces; there will be 32 of them.

Then go through the following process:

1. Shuffle the cards thoroughly.

2. Cut them with your left hand.

3. Deal out 13 cards, face up.

4. Pick out the Aces and set them aside.

5. Return the cards (except for the Aces) to the deck.

Go through the process two more times.

Your answer depends on the number of Aces you have set aside. If you have all 4 of them, the answer is yes. If all 4 came up in the first deal, it is a resounding yes. Chances are slimmer with fewer Aces.

Apple Twist

 # OF PLAYERS: 1 OR more

YOU NEED:
an apple with a stem for each person

Twist the stem once for each letter of the alphabet. Where the stem falls off is the initial of your true love.

Daisy, Daisy

YOU NEED:
a daisy

This is an old variation on the classic "he-loves-me-he-loves-me-not" theme. You pluck the petals off a daisy one by one with each line. Just start again (if you need to) when you finish plucking off the 12th petal.

One I love
Two I love
Three I love I say
Four I love with all my heart
And five I cast away.
Six he loves

Seven she loves
Eight they both love
Nine he comes
Ten he tarries
Eleven he courts
And twelve he marries.

Love, Marriage, and Luck with Dominoes

This ancient method of telling fortunes is limited. You can only do it once a month, and never on Friday or Monday. When you can do it, you may only draw 3 dominoes at a sitting. Break the rules and the answers will be "wrong."

Shuffle the dominoes around on the table, face down, before selecting one. Before you select a second domino, shuffle them around again.

If you select:

6-6: You will marry someone rich and have many children.

6-5: Don't be discouraged. Even if the person you love rejects you, you will eventually succeed.

6-4: Early marriage and much happiness.

6-3: Love, happiness, riches, and honors.

6-2: Happy marriage, luck in business, bad luck for thieves.

6-1: Two marriages. The second one will be happier.

6-blank: Loss of a friend.

5-5: Luck. Success, but not necessarily money.

5-4: Not good for money matters. You will marry someone poor or someone who has expensive tastes.

5-3: Comfortable marriage. You will never be poor.

5-2: Misfortune in love. If you marry the one you love, it may not work out in the long run. For a female: a good life, if you stay single.

5-1: You will receive an invitation and you will enjoy yourself very much. Not good for money matters.

5-blank: For a female: sorrow through the affections. For a male: difficult financial conditions.

4-4: An invitation (to a party?) at which you will have a wonderful time.

4-3: You will marry young and live happily.

4-2: A big change in your life. If you quarrelled with a friend, you will make up and be better friends than before.

4-1: Happy marriage.

4-blank: Bad for love affair. This foretells quarrels and separations. Don't tell your secret; it won't be kept.

3-3: Riches.

3-2: Good for love and travel.

3-1: Secret love affairs.

3-blank: Invitation (to a party?) at which you will meet someone new. If you marry: difficult mate.

2-2: Success in love. Happiness in marriage. Success, but not necessarily money.

2-1: For a female, you will marry young and live a life of luxury. For a male, lucky in love.

2-blank: Bad luck. For females: good luck if you live alone. Safe voyage. Possible accident, but protection against physical injury.

1-1: Affection and happiness in love and marriage.

1-blank: Loss of money. Sorrow in love.

Blank-blank: Sorrow in love. Disappointment.

How to Tell Your Luck with Dice

YOU NEED:
    3 dice
    a dice cup or box
    a board
    a piece of chalk

PREPARATION:
Draw a chalk circle on the board.

This method of telling fortunes is less restricted than the domino method, but it also has its limitations. You may not use it on days that are unlucky for dice—Mondays and Wednesdays.

    Put the dice in the dice cup and shake it with your left hand. Then throw the dice into the chalk circle. You read the message by counting the number of spots on the top of the three dice and checking the total in the following list.

    If you throw:

3: Success in love. Many relationships.
4: Many relationships, but you will not be perfectly pleased with any of them.
5: Obstacles and quarrels in love. If you're going on a trip, some disagreeable incident will take place, but it won't be serious.
6: Many relationships, exciting life.
7: Luck in money matters.

8: Stinginess. Whoever throws it will never be poor, but may live poorly through miserliness.

9: Good luck in everything, except games of chance.

10: Good luck. If a young girl throws this, she will not marry soon, but will have good luck in other matters. If a married woman throws it, she may get a legacy. If a man throws it, he will have good luck in love.

11: Extravagance. Waste of money.

12: An event of some kind—happy or unhappy. Has nothing to do with matters of love.

13: Be alert. People around you may not be trustworthy.

14: If a female throws it, unhappy marriage. Good life if she stays single. For a man: dishonesty, lack of principles.

15: Bad luck in speculation. Good luck in marriage.

16: Bad luck in business. Good luck in marriage.

17: You won't find the property you lost. Good luck in your work. Disappointment otherwise.

18: Riches, honors, a happy life. Good luck in love and in your work. Bad luck for thieves.

If you get the same number twice, you will get news from someone far away.

If you throw the dice out of the chalk circle, don't bother to count the totals. It means you will have a quarrel.

If the dice fall on the floor, it will be a violent quarrel.

If one die lands on top of the other, the answer is negative.

Four Kings— Four Queens

OF PLAYERS: I OR more

YOU NEED:
> an ordinary deck of playing cards

Here is another "Who loves me?" game.

Set up four playing cards—all Kings—in a row horizontally. If you want to find out about women, use all Queens.

Assign the cards names, so that each King or Queen represents a different person. The King of Hearts, for example, might be Tony; the King of Diamonds, Gary; the King of Clubs, Alan; and the King of Spades, someone you haven't met yet— or a specific name, if you want.

Then the questions start. The first question might be: "Which one is in love with me?" You start dealing out the deck, laying the cards face up, starting with the King of Hearts, placing each card halfway up on each King. The first card that agrees in suit with the King it is placed upon indicates the answer to your question.

If, for example, you deal a Jack of Clubs onto the King of Hearts, you go on to the next card. A 6 of Spades on the King of Diamonds? On to the next card. A 5 of Clubs on the King of Clubs—there is your answer: Alan is in love with you.

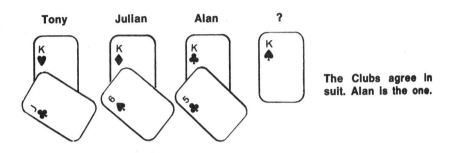

The Clubs agree in suit. Alan is the one.

If you don't get a matchup after dealing four cards, go on to deal another card—or two, or however many it takes.

Continue to ask questions, all of them beginning with "Which one?" Each question is answered as soon as the suits agree.

My Fortune

 # OF PLAYERS: 2 OR MORE

YOU NEED:
paper and pencil

You make up this game yourself to suit the players. It's great for sleepovers, but you can also design it for parties by using different questions and answers.

Write down the questions you and your group would be most interested in, or would laugh at the most. You could have:

1. What will I be when I grow up?
2. Who will I work with?
3. What will they call me?
4. Where will I live?
5. What is the most exciting thing I'll ever do?
6. Who will I marry?
7. How old will I be when I get married?
8. Where will we go for our honeymoon?
9. What will I do for fun?
10. What will be my greatest achievement?

The possibilities of course are endless. Take a large sheet of paper, divide it into boxes about 3 inches (7.5 cm) square, and write one question at the top of each box. (Or use a new page in a notebook, instead of a box, for each question.) Below each question write a list of appropriate, humorous, and just plain silly answers—and number them.

For example, some answers to question #10 might be:

1. Staying awake.
2. Remembering your address.
3. Getting the bubble gum off your face.
4. Learning to belly dance.

Once you have at least six answers for every question, you'll be ready to tell anyone's (well, almost anyone's) fortune. Simply read the first question and ask the player to choose a number from 1 to 6 (or however many answers you have for that question). When the player says a number, read the corresponding answer.

Love, Friendship, Marriage, Hate

To test your compatibility with another person, match up your names like this:

> C L A R I S S A   B E D L I N G T O N
> R O B E R T   H U G H   M E R I V A L E

Then strike out the letters that are the same in each name, like this:

> C ~~L~~ A ~~R~~ I S S ~~A~~   ~~B E D~~ L ~~I~~ N ~~G T O~~ N
> R ~~O B E R T~~   H U ~~G~~ H   M E R ~~I~~ V ~~A L E~~

What is left is:

> C A I S S D L N N

and:

> R H U H M E R V E

Now start reading off "Love, Friendship, Marriage, Hate," for the letters that are left, as follows:

> "Love (C), Friendship (A), Marriage (I), Hate (S),
> Love (S), Friendship (D), Marriage (L), Hate (N),
> Love (N)."

Therefore, Clarissa loves Robert. Let's see how he feels about her:

"Love (R), Friendship (H), Marriage (U), Hate (H),
Love (M), Friendship (E), Marriage (R), Hate (V),
Love (E)."

Isn't that convenient?

You can use this same compatibility tester for schools you're thinking of going to or companies you're thinking of working for, and so on.

Reading Tea Leaves

YOU NEED:

> a cup of tea that has been brewed from tea leaves, not from a tea bag

You have to use your imagination when you read tea leaves. If you see a pattern that reminds you of a mask, for example, you might announce that the person is going to get a part in a play, or be invited to a costume party (especially if you know that one is coming up). You could get very psychological and say that the person is hiding his or her real self.

If you see a door, you could say there will be a change—old doors closing and new ones opening up. If the specks remind you of a kangaroo, you might advise looking before leaping, or moving rapidly—in leaps and bounds—to a goal.

Don't be afraid to make up vague nonsense. It may sound silly to you, but your friends will take it very seriously. Because of that, you need to be careful not to go around scaring people. Keep your predictions happy ones.

Here are a few symbols that you can keep in mind for the times when you really don't see much in the cup.

Anchor: Good results from your plan.
Clover Leaf: Good luck. If it is at the top of the cup as you look at it, the luck is coming soon. If it is at the bottom, there will be a delay.
Clouds: If they are thick, your plans will be delayed. If the clouds are light, good results.

Cross: If it is at the top of the cup, without clouds around it, good luck is coming soon. If at the bottom, troubles over which you will triumph are coming.

Dog: At the top, faithful friends. If surrounded by clouds and dashes, a false friend. At the bottom: be careful not to make anyone jealous or you'll be sorry.

Flower: If at the top or in the middle of the cup, you have or will have a good marriage. If it is at the bottom, anger.

Letter: In the clear, you'll have good news soon. With dots around it, money is coming. Hemmed in by clouds, bad news.

Moon: If it is clear, high honors; if it is clouded over, disappointment that will pass. If at the bottom of the cup, good fortune.

Mountains: One mountain signifies powerful friends. More than one—powerful enemies. If they are clear, friends who have authority.

Snake: At the top or in the middle: if you act honorably, your enemies will not triumph over you. If surrounded by clouds, watch your temper and your actions carefully to avoid trouble.

Star: Happiness. With dots around it: good fortune.

Sun: Luck and happiness. Surrounded by dots, a great change in your life.

Tree: Good health. A group of trees wide apart: you will get your wish. With dashes around them: your good luck has already begun. With dots: riches.

Two-Faced Test

YOU NEED:
> pencil and paper for each player

A test of your friends' psychic abilities? A "free association" test? Neither! It's a hilarious way to tell silly fortunes. Ask your friends to concentrate. You will announce a category and they are to write down the first thought that comes to mind.

1. Name of a person in the room (or movie or rock star)
2. Peculiar human quality
3. Odd place
4. Embarrassing activity
5. Item of apparel that you wear under your clothes
6. Your least favorite song
7. Length of time
8. Something it takes two to do
9. Bad habit
10. Destructive act

When your friends have finished writing down their answers, read off the real questions, which are:

1. What is the name of your secret lover?
2. What does he/she see in you?
3. Where did you meet?
4. What were you doing?
5. What were you wearing?
6. What was the orchestra playing?
7. How long has this been going on?
8. What do you do most of the time when you're alone?
9. What is likely to break it up?
10. What are you going to do next?

Card Games for One

The solitaire games in this section are some of the world's best. What makes them so good?

Every one of them has something about it that is intriguing and challenging, and that makes it especially fun to play. There are no dull, tedious games here. All of them are mesmerizing. Once you start playing them, you won't want to stop. They are also practical. You won't find layouts that are too big for your table or call for three or four decks of cards. The ratio between the number of cards you have to lay out and the amount of action in the game is usually a comfortable one. You won't have to lay out two packs of cards only to discover that the game is lost before you get to make a move!

Also, these are less well-known games. You probably already know how to play the famous ones like Klondike and Canfield.

Have fun with them!

Accordion

This game is also called Methuselah, the Tower of Babel, and the Idle Year.

Start by dealing the cards one at a time face up in a row of four from left to right. Go slowly so that you can keep comparing the cards you deal with their neighbors. Whenever a card matches the card on its left—or third to its left—you move the new card over onto the one it matches. The match may be in suit or rank.

Let's say that the first four cards you turn up are:

The 8 of Spades matches the 8 of Clubs (on its left) and also the 5 of Spades (third to its left). You could move it onto either one. Which one will turn out better? You really can't tell at this point.

Once you move a card over, though, the card on the bottom doesn't have any significance. The card on top is the one to match.

As soon as you move a card—or a pile—move the later cards over to close up the sequence. That will open up new moves for you, too.

Go on dealing cards, one at a time, stopping after each one to make whatever moves are possible, until you've used up all the cards.

For example, suppose that you deal:

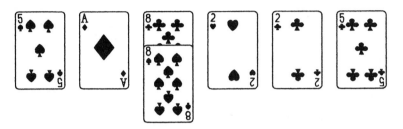

You can move the 2 of Clubs onto the 2 of Hearts. Then close up the row. The 5 of Clubs moves next to the 2s. It's a Club and that's a match! But once you move the 5 over onto the 2 of Clubs, another move opens up. You can move the entire pile over onto the 5 of Spades, which is the third card to the left. So the cards look like this:

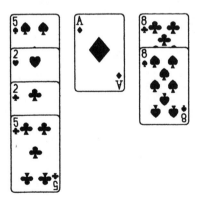

To win the game: Get the whole pack into one pile. It's almost impossible. If you end up with five piles, you're doing pretty well!

The Clock

This game is also known as Hidden Cards, Sundial, Four of a King, All Fours, Travelers, and Hunt.

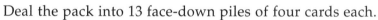

Deal the pack into 13 face-down piles of four cards each.

Arrange 12 of them in a circle, representing the numbers on a clock face. Put the 13th pile in the middle of the circle. It should look like this:

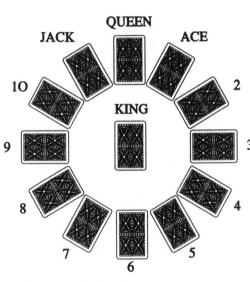

Start by picking up the top card of the center pile. Suppose it is a 5. Slip it, face up, under the card pile in the five o'clock position. Then pick up the top card from that pile. Suppose it is a Jack. It would go under the 11 o'clock pile (remember, the King pile is in the middle of the clock, and the Queen is at 12). Then you would pick up the top card of the 11 o'clock pile and slip it under whatever pile it belongs in.

When you slip the fourth card of any group into place—and there is no face-down card to turn over—turn over the top card of the next highest card pile.

To win the game: Get all the cards turned face up before the fourth King is turned face up.

The Wish

If you win this game the first time you try it, you will get your wish—or so they say.

Use a deck of 32 cards by discarding all cards from the 2s through the 6s. Shuffle them well and then count off four cards at a time face down. Then turn them face up. Be careful to keep the pile squared up so that you cannot see what any of the cards are below the top.

Deal the whole deck into piles of four cards in the same way.

Then lift off the top cards in pairs of the same kind—two 7s, two Queens, and so on. Keep going as long as you see any pairs.

To win the game: Clear away all the cards in pairs.

Four-Leaf Clover

You will have good luck all day if you win this game, they say.

Discard all four 10s from the deck. You won't be using them at all. Shuffle the remaining 48 cards well. Then deal 16 cards face up on the table in four rows of four cards each.

Whenever you can, throw out from these rows any two or more cards of the same suit. These can be (1) two or more cards that total 15 each, such as 9 and 6, or 8, 4, 2, and Ace (Ace counts as 1) or (2) the King, Queen, and Jack of the same suit.

After you throw out a batch of cards, deal from the deck to fill the spaces left in the 16-card layout.

To win the game: Throw out all 48 cards (the whole deck).

TIP:
In making 15s, try to remove as many cards as possible, so as to bring in as many new cards as possible. For example, when you have a choice, remove an Ace and a 2 rather than a 3.

Miss Milligan

To many people, this is the ultimate solitaire game. You need two decks of cards for it.

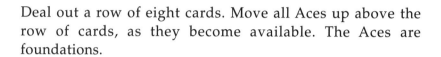

Deal out a row of eight cards. Move all Aces up above the row of cards, as they become available. The Aces are foundations.

Besides building on the foundations, you can build within the original row of eight cards—downward in alternating colors.

When you've made all possible moves, deal out another eight cards that overlap the original eight, filling in spaces as you go.

Play off what you can to the foundations, build what you can on the row, and deal another eight cards onto the layout.

Continue this process until you've used up all the cards in your hand. At this point you have the option of "weaving."

WEAVING

This is the option of removing one card from the bottom row of the layout temporarily—while you make other moves. When you get that card back into play—either on a foundation or on the layout—you are then allowed to remove another card. You can keep doing this until you win the game or until you can't find a place for the card.

SPECIAL RULES

You are permitted to move two or more cards as a unit—when they are built correctly in rank and sequence and at the end of a column. For example, in the diagram below, you can move the 10 of Diamonds, 9 of Spades, and 8 of Hearts as a unit onto the Jack of Clubs.

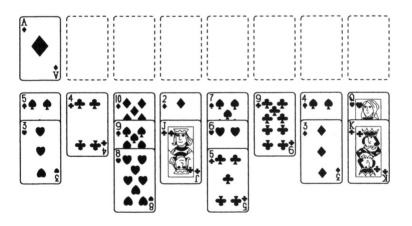

Spaces may be filled with any available King or with a sequence that leads off with a King.

Answers

BRAIN BAFFLERS

1. Dolores is taller than Emily, who is taller than Ann.

2. Yes, as long as the other half are male, too. She has five sons.

3. He will need twenty 9s: one each for the numbers 9, 19, 29, 39, 49, 59, 69, 79, 89, 90, 91, 92, 93, 94, 95, 96, 97, and 98; and two for 99.

4. At each stop, passengers can buy a ticket for any of the 24 remaining stops. Therefore, the number of tickets will be 25 x 24 = 600.

5. Let's imagine that the inhabitants are as different as possible (one will be bald, another will have only one hair, another two, another three, and so on, until we get to someone having 100,000 hairs). Inhabitant #100,002 will have the same number of hairs as someone among the first 100,001 inhabitants. The total population is more than 200,000 people, which means that there will be more than 100,000 inhabitants with the same number of hairs as other people in town.

6. Lisa has one red, one blue, and one green scarf.

7. Two blankets, each one inch thick, will be warmer because the air beneath them also acts as insulation.

8. There are 6 chestnut trees per side, making a total of 12.

9. Twelve muffins. When Amy ate half the remaining muffins plus three more to leave none, she must have eaten six muffins. So Jennifer ate half the muffins and left six, meaning that there were twelve to start with.

10. Hairdressers don't cut their own hair. Therefore, the clean hairdresser gave the bad haircut and the dirty hairdresser gave the perfect haircut. Thus it is better to go to the dirty salon.

11. First he immersed the crown in a container of water and measured the level of the water. Then he removed the crown and immersed the gold bar, measuring the water level. The levels were not the same, so therefore the gold had been mixed with another metal.

12. He took out one marble and swallowed it before anybody could see its color. This forced the count to take out the other marble. It was black, of course, so they all assumed that the previous one had been white.

13. A bird cannot fly on the moon because there is no air to suspend it.

14. There are only three people: a daughter, her mother, and her grandmother. The mother received 25 books from the grandmother, and then gave 8 of them to her daughter.

15. If Albert had stopped the cassette player when the killer came in, the tape would not have been rewound. This means that the killer had listened to the tape to make sure that the imitation was perfect.

16. The maid is lying, because pages 99 and 100 are two sides of the same sheet of paper.

17. Bicycles.

18. He made each candidate ride another candidate's horse. Each one would of course try to come in first, because in that way the owner of the horse that a particular candidate was riding would lose the race.

19. New York City is in the Northern Hemisphere and Australia is in the Southern. Due to the earth's movement, water and air masses turn in different directions in both hemispheres. In the Southern

Hemisphere they turn clockwise; in the Northern, counterclockwise. When she saw the direction of the water draining from the sink, she knew where she was.

20. The footprints were not very deep, which means that they could not have belonged to a very heavy person. Therefore, they had to belong to the secretary, who had changed shoes to hide her crime. Both wounds must have occurred when the victim placed a hand on his chest before the gunshot, and the bullet crossed his hand before going into his body.

21. She should pour it before going upstairs, because the coffee will lose more heat before adding the milk than after. (Matter loses heat proportionately to the difference in temperature with the environment.)

22. 29 days. One spider would have covered half of the space on the 29th day, and on the 30th day would repeat what had been done, covering the space completely. Two spiders would each have covered half the space in 29 days, therefore covering the entire area.

23. Before leaving home, Dan wound the clock and set it for 12:00. When he got back home, he knew exactly how long he had been out from his own clock. At Lee's house, he had checked the time. Once he was home, he subtracted the time he was at Lee's from the total time indicated by the clock. The remainder was used in walking to and from Lee's house. He divided this number by two and added the result to the time that he saw on his friend's clock when he was leaving.

24. 3 x 75 = 225 qualities distributed among 100 persons, so at least 25% of them have all three.

25. Two turns on itself. Try it.

Index